Let Your Heart Talk

by Dale Grant Stephens

Heart Talk
Productions

Dale Grant Stephens, Poet, Writer and Photographer

What others say

To my father
Who has guided me and granted me the wisdom of his journeys.
Who has taught me courage and built the nest from which my strong independent spirit has flown, who continues to be a source of inspiration and pleasure to make proud.
Always your daughter.   *Amber*, 15/12/2000

Dear Dale,

   As I reflect on the letter to your daughter it brings tears to my eyes. It touched my heart and soul especially not having a father for twenty years. Thank you for the opportunity to have met you and spent special moments together. Everything does happen for a reason and I know why at this moment in my life I met you. I am so very clear on my values – on my no compromise list, more than ever before. Human beings are so complex – heart, soul, feelings, emotions, values, beliefs, opinions etc. Much more than skin deep!

   Well Dale, your kind words of support and encouragement and the opportunity to read some of your precious work has really assisted my continued development and left a huge impact on my life. Thank you and let's keep in touch. Keep safe and enjoy the moments
Best wishes,
Helena x
Head of Ground staff (An Australian Airline) 1999

The beauty of age is wisdom and experience harvested to feed the young. *Amber Stephens*, 2002

From our first meeting I was so inspired by Dale's ability to convey a vision. He encouraged and coached us on how we could all be masters of our own destiny. After working for Dale I have progressed to the position of Regional Product Manager for Kodak Asia Pacific. It is my sincere belief, that without Dale's influence in my life, I would never have reached the position I now hold. It is rare to find mentors these days. Dale has continued as a friend I respect. He has been and always will be a mentor to me.
Richard Fleming, General Manager Kodak Products, Asia Pacific 2001

I was married to Dale for 15 years. Four years after our separation I worked for Dale as a qualified financial planner. I therefore know him from a personal and business point of view as well as the role of father of our children. I offered to write this out of respect for Dale as a person and in the sincere belief that Dale has very special qualities. He is an emotionally mature caring person. He is also an astute businessman, skilled in communication and well versed in the principals of investment. In his presentation of seminars, he commands respect trust and confidence. He has also succeeded as a parent and I know his children both love and respect him. He is also their confidant and friend. People remark on our enduring friendship, after 10 years apart he still remains one of my best friends and confidants.
Barbara E Derrett, 1998

Dale's wisdom derives from the turning of the seasons of his life. Having enjoyed wealth, loss, pain and the rewards of success, he faced a life-threatening illness nearly dying on two occasions and lived to benefit. He gained a greater appreciation of the simple pleasures that bring inner peace and contentment. Writing from the heart, he is fearless in his willingness to sensitively and insightfully say what many of us feel. Such writing can only be drawn from the well of personal experience backed by the courage of conviction born of solitude and reflection.
Eddie Rayner, foundation member of Split Enz

First Published in December 2003
Second Printing June 2004
Third Printing July 2005

Heart Talk Productions
PO Box 42 207, Orakei, Auckland 1130
Email: bookorders@hearttalk.co.nz
Website: www.hearttalk.co.nz

ISBN 0-476-00195-1

Production by the Bannochburn Trust
Print Management by Graphic Resource
Book layout by Claire O'Connor
Production House: Heart Talk Productions

POETRY and PROSE by Dale Grant Stephens
PHOTOGRAPHY by Dale Grant Stephens
Photos on pages 9 and 31 by courtesy of friends.

The sequel to *Let Your Heart Talk* will be available in October 2005.
Those wanting copies please email us at bookorders@hearttalk.co.nz

Foreword

Life has taught me that irrespective of age, race, culture and upbringing, we the human race, all desire much the same things from life: To give and receive love, to be respected and accepted.

We all desire to live in a world free of fear and to retain our dignity. We also seek fulfilment at work and to feel we are valued for whom we really are. Personal freedom, inner peace coupled with good mental and physical health are the foundations upon which we hope to build our lives. Most of us dare to believe that these life goals are attainable.

However, the reality is often in stark contrast to our youthful expectations. It is then we need encouragement, sagely advice and a word in season. My journey has introduced me to the vagaries of the seasons.

Perhaps the greatest good that comes out of loss, is that one recognises that excessive time spent in the pursuit of wealth and prestige denies us time for those things which bring richness to the human spirit. A lack of balance can cause us to lose those things that are at the core of human happiness. Our peace of mind and our relationships suffer.

I was inspired to write this book because of the lack of mentors in our society, who in earlier generations offered sagely advice? People of my generation should pause in the autumn of life and look back with compassion on those following.

Some lessons are only learnt at great cost. However, having spent 25 years as a financial advisor listening to and advising hundreds of family members, I know that so much pain and loss could have been avoided.

This book is for all of you on this journey of life. It is distilled from seven years of reflective writing. I offer it in all humility because as the proverb says "I became a fool that I may be truly wise". My verse is from the heart and a lifetime of learning. I trust where will be a word in season for you.

I know that words read and spoken have a direct influence on our lives. What we speak is what we get because our speech reflects our inner thoughts. Hence "as you think so shall you be". So please drink from this cup and pass it on to a fellow traveller.

Sincerely,

Dale

Index

From One Heart to Another

In human wisdom, the mentor relays knowledge
Knowing that he or she is also still a pupil
Until such time as we can "walk the talk" we remain the pupil
In that respect I am still a student of life

Dale Grant Stephens

Let Your Heart Talk is a book of refreshing words that travel from heart to heart.

The demands of every day life allow too little time for reflection
that enables us to listen to our inner voice and ask where to now?
Am I following my dreams? Is this the best pathway to my goals?

We are bombarded with the written word like inane chatter
So little time for beautiful thoughts and words of inspiration
Every so often we discover a reservoir of refreshing words
They travel from heart to heart
They are the songs of the heart, they remind us of what is precious
They clarify what we should avoid, leave behind or caste aside
These words strengthen our resolve and are food on life's journey
They counter negativity and disappointment
because they give life and hope
Empowering and encouraging the heart to speak.

Let Your Heart Talk

If you listen carefully you will hear your heart talk
as it did so many years ago when you were but a child

In those brief years between total dependency and
adult responsibility, you were free with your thoughts and dreams

Your hope soared like an eagle
Your world was exciting and ripe with promise

Then the grey clouds of responsibility and reality
appeared over your valley of hope

They blocked out the sun and you felt the chill of change
Other people's voices and expectations drowned out the sound
of your own heart and it lost its voice

Now it's time to pause in life to claim back your hope
For your heart wants to speak again
Don't wait until it's a forlorn whisper in the twilight of life
Seek a sweet valley of tranquillity away from the pace.
Then sit and think, have I drifted from the path of my dreams?
Listen carefully and you will hear faintly at first
the gentle soft voice of your heart calling in the stillness of the night
"Do you still care? Do you dare to hope again?"

Now search your inner thoughts
Listen to your heart and the whisper will become
the sound of a gentle brook and hope will rise from within.
Then you will hear the roar of a mighty river
You have heard once more the voice of reason
echoing off the walls of your soul
Your dreams are riding in on hope to meet you
for your heart has spoken once again

Why don't I do as you say
Why do I no longer let you think my thoughts?

Listen, my heart is trying to speak, sssh …
Listen can't you hear it whispering in the wind along the street?

Talking sense and recompense and how I really feel

It is the truth drifting towards me over the fields of broken dreams
A voice I couldn't hear when in pursuit of fruitless schemes

Reminding me of who I am and who I want to be
It said, "Now you are listening, let us talk of how to set you free."

Dare to Learn

I have walked amidst the sorrows of my youth
as I came to terms with universal truth.
There is freedom when listening to my heart
If in error I have walked, then in life I've played a part.
Mistakes have taught me, I am wiser now than I was at the start.

Forgiveness

When I forgave myself and ceased to blame,
When I realised mistakes are the leaves along my path.
Mistakes lost their shame.
I had the freedom and courage to try again
To know that in growing we must sometimes fail
Yet there will be a happier tale,
Provided we remember the lessons and forget the pain.
Focus on what we have achieved and be proud of the gain.
Forgive others too, knowing that they are human like me and you.

Life Is This Moment

Life is this moment no more or less
So this moment of all moments is the most precious.
The past is very interesting and informative,
but it does not warrant our focus
It has fallen like leaves to the soil, see it as such.
Keep only the fruit from the harvest
Recognise the fruit from past seasons,
being the lessons and the good memories
They enrich this moment, please our thoughts and are ours to keep.

Lessons learnt guide us past the land mines on our journey
The future will always be the future and as such has no reality.
However, our activities and thoughts are the architects of our tomorrow.
So we design our future with our predominant thoughts
Therefore, be selective,
choose wisely what you allow to dwell in your mind.
Choose seeds of thought as if you are planting for tomorrow
Decide what reflects your maturity and hope
knowing the crop is always true to the seed
Tomorrow you will be a product of what you think and do today.
So think your way to your future and speak your hope,
'life and death are in the power of the tongue'
visualise yourself as you wish to be then act out the person you want to be
In so doing you allow your mind to find the pathway to your dreams.

Me Being Me, You Being You

I've joined the few who dared to take a path they never knew,
We've learned to re-think and question, Why?
To listen to the other point of view,
To let go of outdated dreams, irrelevant schemes
To see the folly of standing in line without questioning, Why?
or towing, the line, wanting to be different but not to try.

I realise it's not a question of being different for difference sake,
That it is cowardliness in society to conform, just for peer group sake.

Now I look afresh at life each day
Knowing I have a right to decide what I want in my life
To decide where and when.
Because where there is a will there is a way.

Walk With Me

Learn life's principles from nature its itself.
Stop and study the natural world
Come walk with me on a ridge or wild windswept beach

Note the character of the pohutakawa
A tree whose beauty reflects the severity of the climate
That moulds gracefully to reflect the vagaries of the seasons
See also the rugged beauty and tenacity of her exposed root system
Sensuously feeling its way down the cliff
over boulders, seeking water and earth

Stand for a while in a high wind or gale
See this mighty tree sway in unison with the forces of nature
It is the very hardship, which has created her strength and beauty
Her shape embodies the turbulence and reflects the seasons

Look into the face of those that have suffered.
They who have survived with their values intact
You will recognise the same beauty and strength.
Character was never born of ease
If you should doubt me, pause on your way home
Visit a sheltered garden, nursery or park
See the soft pretty and perfect trees
They are products of an unnaturally sheltered world.

Beauty Born of Hardship

Because you have not been born of ease
You have endurance and persistence within.
Because you have grown through adversity
You are the personification of that gnarled tree
Whose beauty empowers and gives inspiration.

You Have Earned It

Be encouraged there is a positive side of your suffering.
It is the inner strength waiting to be exercised
You see, no one can buy your fortitude and character.
This comes from all those years of suffering

This inner strength is yours
It is reinforcing steel that will support your future
Decide what it is you want from life,
Plan how you intend to achieve it.
Visualise yourself in receipt of your goal
Then apply persistence and determination
The very qualities that have sustained you
in trials and tribulation.
These are your core strengths that will empower you,
enabling you to claim what is rightfully yours.

The body consists almost entirely of water
We can be like water lying in a puddle
or become the wave that inspires
and expresses the strength that lies within.

The Reward of Tenacity

The rich flavour and subtle tastes of life's treasures
Are yielded from the extremes of the seasons.
Given strength by the winters of trial and need.
Baked in the heat of adversity, the clay builds its durable strength.
Only out of contrast and lack can one truly appreciate
How fantastic are the simple pleasures.
How satisfying is the reward of perseverance and courage.
Without a degree of humility and understanding
We cannot relate with compassion to the less fortunate.
Because our need, our trials and overcoming produces
The character and strength that recognises true riches.
It is what allows us to slip free of pride and prejudice
To find pleasure in what so many take for granted
To see that true wealth is measured in the richness of relationships.

Loss or Gain

Money has wings, fame, but a short life.
When you are money centred and you lose everything,
you have very little left that you value.
When you have a firm set of values that reflects the best of the human spirit
and if you also retain your true friends and loving relationship with family,
you retain that which is at the core of human happiness.
You are then free from the selfish demands made by excessive acquisition,
you are able to focus on relationships and enjoy friends.
Nurture your relationships and you'll gain wealth in the human spirit.

You don't have to own the playground to enjoy the swings.

Parted But Not Separated

Some say that each parting is a kind of death,
when it leaves us in doubt as to whether we shall meet again.

We should remember, that the very current of life that brought us together
is the same life force on which we part to continue this journey through life.
This very same current will bring new friends and experience into our lives

So just as one year makes way for another; a parting of friends,
makes time for new friendships.
Hence there is both joy and sorrow in parting.

Like the rings on the cross-section of the trunk of a tree,
good friends who come and go, leave an indelible mark on the seasons of our life.

Human will and destiny have the power to reunite old friends.
However, if circumstances, obligations or death should separate us for life,
realise that positive relationships of the past are interwoven into who we are.

Each significant relationship, has contributed to our learning and growing
Meaningful relationships are an indelible part of the fibre of our being.
As such they become part of what we think and who we are.
Time spent with such friends can never be stolen or lost.

The Gift of Knowing You

Farewell, but not goodbye.
Fly away my friend but never from my memory.

If we do not meet again on the journey of life,
thank *you* for the gift of knowing *you*.
Share my faith, that when compatible spirits meet,
Our spirits will recognise each other in the transit to life after death
and what a reunion that will be.

Evolving

The fullness of life is to feel, to express, to experience and to grow.
It is important to understand early on in life's journey
the purpose and balance that makes life worthwhile to be.
To truly live, is to understand the possibilities.
To seek to fulfil one's potential according to one's real needs and desires.
For each one of us to experience the fullness of living
each of us must choose from a multitude of choices, the path we take.
Sometimes change is not a choice but it presents us with choices
Knowing what we want is the key to our potential being realised.
Then we need the commitment to attain it.

Remember and accept that change is constant.
Those that fear and resist the inevitable force of change
are resisting their very existence.
I say this because change is the reality of all living things.
One must adapt to survive and grow.
Those that welcome and embrace the inevitability of change,
are flowing with the current of life itself.
Change like the blood that flows through our veins,
bringing fresh nutrients to the mind and soul.
Only then is vitality derived from an inner strength.
Accepting this enables us to approach life with dignity and peace.

When We Change Our Thinking

We are still capable of changing our lives for the better.
Negative people will always seek our company.
They will influence our thoughts
attempting to reinforce our doubts and fears.
If you can't find positive people supportive of your hopes and dreams
Then seek the written word that encourages you to dwell on your hope.
Read books that will implant seeds of positive thought
Dwelling on such revelation is like watering the seed of thought.
This is the power of meditation, that nurtures the realisation of your desires
Each path we take is like a stepping stone
The path may not lead to our ultimate objective
However, it is a finite step to our ultimate goal
It enriches our understanding
enabling us to see more clearly the direction ahead.

Your Hands

Your hands are the extension of your feelings,
they are the sensitive out reaching of your love

They have touched everybody you ever loved
They have caressed and held, reassured measured and steadied
Your hands have expressed what is on your heart.
All your life they have reached out in love and understanding.

It was your hands that cushioned your fall from your first steps.
They have been with you from the womb
and reflect both the years of your life, and your toil.
Your hands have defended you and held on to that which is precious.

They have fed and offered drink,
and dispersed from the generosity of your heart.
They have gladly held all you have ever received,
and willingly given everything you ever gave.

They have borne the weight of all you have ever carried.
They are the road map of your toil.
It is your hands who have defended you and held back your aggressor.
They have warned you of the extremes of both heat and cold.

Through your hands you have understood.
Touched the silky softness of the hair on head
of those you love intimately.
Even in darkness they have led you.

They are with you for life, they are of the expression of you.
That is why I love every line and mark being the evidence
of age and service.
Your hands were the most used and most supportive part of your body.
That is also is why it was so precious when you touched or held me.
It was your hands that taught me as a child.
They have added to my understanding and sensation of things beautiful.

Happiness

Happiness is a frequent visitor to some, and a regular companion for others.
Happiness is the long awaited companion of the mind and heart of people
Courted by money it pays brief visits to many people in various pursuits
But is easily bored by frivolity, it becomes restless and moves on.
It is the frequent companion of those who both give and receive love
because you cannot give from a spirit of love without receiving
It befriends those that care for others, as well as people who know
where they are going in this world and the next.
It tires of selfishness and self-indulgence.
It is attracted to character born of making choices that align with our values and ethics.
There is no quick fix platitudinous method of achieving it.
It is found when we pause to count our blessings and help others on their journey
It appears when we change direction in response to the voice
of our inner integrity and need.

There are some situations and people it avoids, such as those who are
too stressed and driven by conformity to have time for personal pursuits.
It is not found in a big pot at the end of the rainbow either:
It is found in little pieces along the pathway to where we are going
Your happiness is ultimately dependent on being at peace with yourself
You will have inner strength and satisfaction from character choices
This is the core of self respect and the foundation of inner peace
I say this because happiness is an "inside" feeling.

Achievement

Timeless wisdom prevails at the end of the day
Happiness comes from balancing wisdom
with what your heart has to say.
Achievement is propelled by a burning desire
Then it is perseverance that feeds that fire.
Try to recognise that fear will steal every worthwhile goal
But in reality fear steals only five percent of what people really need.
Fear wins when it prevents us from following our dreams.
Goals need to be written down and viewed each day
Because contemplation and meditation both prepare the way.
Success is best shared and often results from people working in teams
It combines talent and energy: there is added pleasure in shared dreams.
Reassess your goals with the changing perspective of your lives
This is how the energy to achieve survives.
Your dreams gain purpose with meditation.
Coupled with the power of visualisation.
Goals are also empowered by faith and prayer
Both bring your future expectations near.
What we say is what we get:
Negative statements give life to your fear and regret.
Life and death are in the power of the tongue
What people say effects everyone.
The enemy of your dreams and goals is procrastination
The main reason people never reach their destination.

Dream-stealers suck power from us all
So eliminate them from your life or they will cause you to fall.
Continued lack of sleep and exercise
kills incentive and the ability to rise:
Confidence departs if you're constantly tired.
You'll have about as much motivation as those whose goals have expired.
Tell the world what you are going to do *after* the project is finished and through
For success requires no explanation and failure allows no alibis
It can't be substituted with excuses and lies.
For life is judged by what you do;
To your own self be true.
Remember success or failure is determined by your personal point of view:
It can only be judged by what success is to you.

The Character of Leadership

Freedom also comes when we have the courage to be true to ourselves
Knowing we made a choice in line with our values gives us inner strength.
It supports our self-esteem, forgiving ourselves is essential too
The more we adhere to these principles the stronger we become
When actions reflect values, it radiates as character and leadership
This growth of character brings contentment and is health to the spirit and soul.
This is the quality that is the hall-mark of true leadership.

The Beauty of Age

As the mind matures our youthful desires are trapped in an ageing body.
So the acceptance of an ageing body is a milestone in human understanding.
When physical strength is transformed to the mind and wealth to the spirit,
Then people see beauty in the weathered face of the aged and think:
"There is race well run. Oh to know the half of it!
Such quiet assurance, a knowing
There is the fruit of a mature mind.
The source of contentment, the beauty of character
Pray tell me how did you arrive at this place in your life?"

The doll like beauty of youth can never compete with a character face
Those compassionate eyes, the smile lines, being the maturity of beauty:
Real beauty radiates from within.
Fear and doubt have been replaced by grace
Doubt gives way to assurance and dignity prevails like a mantle.
A quiet knowing where there was once an anxious wondering.

This, my friend, is the reward and beauty of maturity.

The Fruit on the Tree

You are getting older, aren't we all?
The tree has grown
What fruit did it bear?
Who did it shelter?
As the body ages, the mind matures.
In some the mind chooses to follow the body.
In others it goes on alone:
It gains momentum and gathers riches,
It adds dimension to the body
Empowering the human spirit.
Then others recognise the character of the life force within the physical form
That, my friend, is the richness of growing old with grace
Toned with wisdom, blessed with contentment,
Having discovered who you are and what you believe in.
Only then does age have presence and depth.
An alluring radiance best described as a contented knowing.

The Key to Leadership

One person with an idea is a visionary.
When that person has a plan to achieve that vision
She or he has potential waiting to be fulfilled
When the same individual is motivated by desire
that is empowered by conviction, you have a powerful energy.
Apply faith and persistent effort and the dream will become reality
If that same person is able to communicate that vision
with enthusiasm and sincerity
you have a charismatic leader
By delegating and creating synergy of purpose
combined with talents that complement each other,
you have the birth of a movement that will spread from person to person.
When the energy is sustained, it will spread from town to city
to create a momentum that influences a nation.
Nations influence the world.

If you desire to change our world remember it begins with an individual
who has conviction and strength of purpose.
To inspire others you must touch the hearts, desires and emotions of the people
Give them back their vision, fill their hearts with a new purpose:
Then you harness a dormant energy for good.
Ethnic, racial, cultural and religious incompatibility festers and explodes
in direct defiance of mankind's extraordinary evolvement in science and technology.
For science is not a child of the human spirit.
Religion that does not bare the fruits of love and truth is a deception.
Leaders are required who will turn the tide against negative trends.
Only out of love and truth can leadership emerge that will save the human race
Remember that the seed of both the weed and the life-sustaining crop
lie side by side in the fertile soil of the human heart and mind
Just as hate and love, truth and lies, struggle for the dominance in the human spirit.
We must choose which master we serve, to whom we give our affection.
Like all seed it waits deep within our minds to be germinated
Our predominant thoughts are like the rain and sun
They will draw the seed from the darkness of the soil.
What crop have you planted? What seed do you choose to nurture?
If enough people respond to the call we can turn the tide against
these negative attitudes.
It begins with an awareness that we have the choice.
We cannot serve two masters.
Major decisions will require that we declare our loyalty and character.

Seeing God

I see God in the waves, I see him riding in on the storm.
I see him in the sun set and as it rises here at dawn
I see his character in the trees along the shore
In fact he his is visible in nature and everything that I adore
His purity is in the crystal waves curling in the sun
In the summer he uses flowers for romance and you can see he's having fun
I see God the artist using running water through sand to draw.
In the dawn he uses up the colours that he didn't use the night before.
The ever-moving brush plays with colours in the clouds and the sky
He paints to bring pleasure to you and I
With what is left he paint reflections in the sea
The speed with which he works still amazes me
I see his grace as a bird sweeps into sight
I see his depth in the galaxies at night.
His spirit broods in the sea mist and when wind and waves turn to spray
I feel his warmth on my back as I stroll in his creation every day
The moon is his candle that lights the beach for me at night.

It's what makes it so romantic in the soft evening light
At the end of the summer when we finish with our play
He looks at the mess and uses storms to drive our mess away
He brings the rain to cleanse the land.
This feeds the trees and the storms cleanse the sand
Filling the lakes and rivers, providing water for hot showers.
While we snuggle inside, God works away for hours.
The wind cleans the air we breathe, while like spiders, our webs we weave.
Sometimes when he thinks we take it all for granted.
He takes away some of the things we've built and planted
He leaves on the tap and turns up the power.
The land floods and it rains hour after hour
In the middle of a stormy night we feel humble and a little more contrite.
We remember that although man is smart,
He is no match for Gods power and might
Then it's spring and we rejoice again!
Hence out comes the poet's pen
Sometimes we even thank God in prayer and in praise.
Or simply ask him for more fine summer days.

Love Leads

A follower be, but it is leaders who help to set the people free.
Leaders are rising to change the world and the process begins with you and me.
By being willing to serve and adopting a positive point of view,
The right attitude replaces the old with the new.
Average people want to change the world by changing others.
Exceptional people begin by changing themselves
Instead of pointing the finger at sisters and brothers.
The greatest opportunity to change the world and be a leader,
is given to fathers and mothers.

Today's leaders are being called to rise
To open people's spiritual eyes
To separate truth from lies.

They walk the streets of compassion
Beyond socially acceptable structures and people of fashion:
There is in them no need for status,
For they are driven by love, truth and sacrificial passion.

They are revealing ancient wisdom, bringing a balanced point of view.
For nothing written or said is ever new,
It is your passion and timing and willingness to act and speak,
knowing it is up to you to empower the weak.

When individuals rise up with passion to express a positive point of view
The message stimulates thought; like drops of gentle rain,
Every living growing person is refreshed and they too begin to grow again.

The most powerful force for good, is love spread in practical ways:
It touches hearts and even lengthens our days.
Love dissolves loneliness and drives away fear
By dissolving hate it brings peace near.

Leadership begins in the home and community among family and friends.
Put love and tolerance before materialism and following the latest trends.
Be the first to forgive.
Spread love and forgiveness while you still live.
Take a bunch of flowers.
Listen to those you love and don't count the hours.
Smile at a stranger and talk to children again.
Listen to their story, it will help to encourage or ease their pain.
Write a note to people who give you support
As well as those you love and those who taught.
Tell them why you appreciate them;
Their self-esteem will grow again.
Through this action you will reinforce their qualities.

Freedom

We seek personal freedom but do we understand what it really is?
Note that concerns and needs do not give way to freedom:
neither do the seasons of ones life change to accommodate every wish.
The wind still blows, the ice will freeze and the worm will blight our crops;
It is we who must change,
Then we will see that freedom can dwell in harmony with the winter of our need
In abundance and lack is the seed of humility and gratitude
Just as in pain and pleasure, the seed of appreciation sprouts
from hindsight and contrast
It is not work at the expense of pleasure that is the enemy of freedom,
It is the nature of our work
and the lack of balance between work and relaxation,
For pleasure is there, when we choose to work in accordance
with what we believe in and enjoy.

Freedom is only obtainable when we identify what it is that's making us captive.
Is it over indulgence in the pleasure that has lost its magic?
Or are we in the vice grip of control by those who profess to be our benefactors?
Are we seeking fulfilment from outdated goals?
Or flying a flag for a cause we no longer believe in?
Begin by seeing time as a finite commodity, a diminishing resource
Acknowledge your freedom to prioritise.

Divorce yourself from those who would steal your dreams
and lower your self-esteem,
Cast aside outdated habits along with goals that are driven by
conformity and pride,
Confront the shadowy elusion of fear,
Reject the safe and boring
provided that you are not also rejecting your ethics and values
Base your decisions in line with your inner voice
It will align your intended actions with those values and ethics
For peace of mind is the fruit of freedom when you
listen to your inner voice.
You will hear what is coming from your heart, spirit and soul
Then you must have the courage to follow your dreams

Freedom is accepting the vagaries of the seasons
while exercising our confident self-will to achieve and maintain
the degree of balance that destiny and reality permits.

Expressing Love

When all is said and done people share needs in common with everyone.
Human happiness is determined by the quality of our relationships with others
For we are alone once we leave our fathers and mothers.
The world is just a big community of people longing for the same things as you
They want love, peace and happiness too
If people can't love family and friends
Think what message this sends!
So leadership begins in the home
When we stop communicating we feel alone.
From such realisation and positive actions leaders grow
If you greet these words with cynicism and scorn
Seek to understand the hurt from which it was born.
Let it go, there are new seeds to sow
So begin by making sure your house is still a home.
Remember that by being first to give unconditional love,
You will never be alone.

There are many ways to say I love you:
Think of some caring things you can do.
Write a note to your partner and each of your children don't lecture or shout,
Tell them why you love them, it's something they should never doubt.
When you give love and compassion, hearts are strengthened by your touch.
Is this asking too much?

Rocks of Old

Rocks of old I feast my eyes on your beauty and see etched the seasons of a thousand years.
You were here before me, and shall be, long after my ashes mix with the grains of sand that surround you.
I marvel at your individuality: each of you, with your distinctive character, framed by the sand that is birthed from your relationship with the sea.

The sand is the sediment of your being.
It will be your form in ten thousand years.
Everything on this beach is a testimony of the life force of wave upon wave
Relentlessly caressing these shores licking at your strength.
In a storm, they return, to pound your surface, molding, sculpturing
and defining your rugged beauty over the centuries.
Reducing you to sand, so beautiful, the fragments of your soul.

In the cold front, the winds of change sweep in across the Tasman.
The sea broods in a cloak of mist and rain,
Then the winds begin to murmur, causing the ocean to swell and rise
in rhythm
Like a train coming out of a tunnel, the wind roars into being,
Whipping the waves, sending spray from their white caps.
The sea has risen from its slumber.

On the beach, all life senses the pending storm.
The momentary silence changes to an eerie mournful murmur.
The trees feel the force of the wind.
Here it comes, driving the full force of the storm.

Now the black horizon is sweeping towards me.
In the foreground, the sun breaks through the gathering storm clouds
sending slivers of silver light darting across the sea in the path of the storm.
Momentarily the sun captures the islands in the foreground,
silhouetted against the blackness beyond.
I feel the blood surge in my veins, my life force returns,
The gale lashes the coast in squalls,
It shrieks among the rocks and trees searching every nook and cranny
Then at the doors and windows of every Bach, driving the rain before it.

The sea has responded to the call,
The mighty waves have reached the shore, pounding relentlessly,
tossing and churning.
Even greater rocks rumble as boulders roll.
Each wave claws back more sand to undercover rocks of a thousand years,
Sculptured and sanded by a million tides. Treasure revealed.

I am braced, on the cliffs above the beach, my arms wrapped around a mighty
Pohutakawa feeling the coarse bark against my cheek,
I embrace its spirit of fortitude,
In such moments, I feel the closeness of God as I am supported by his creation.

The wind driven surf whips at my face, I blink to find sight and hold on tight
feeling the surge of excitement as I watch the sea pounding below me.
I am spellbound, as the white foaming waves crash again and again.
The boulders growl as they rumble back and forth, disturbed from their rest
once more.

A lone seagull sweeps in from sea driven before the storm,
like a paper dart in the wind.

A mixture of rain and sea spray penetrates my clothing.
But I am riding a high on the spirit of the storm.
Once again at one with nature.
Having glimpsed the greatest power on earth,
The troubles of the world fade into better perspective.

I see more clearly the frailty of man;
Once more my resolve is strengthened to honour the natural world,
to remember the lessons nature teaches.
All of life's trivial pursuits and conditioned concerns, are swept away,
Here in my human frailty I see the futility of pointless pursuit.

Once more a storm has made mockery of man's dominion over the earth.
For nature at its whim can pull down the temples,
disrupt the strongest economies and reduce mortal man to a state of fear and awe.
These storms always leave me with a sense of wonder, invigorated,
released and high on living.

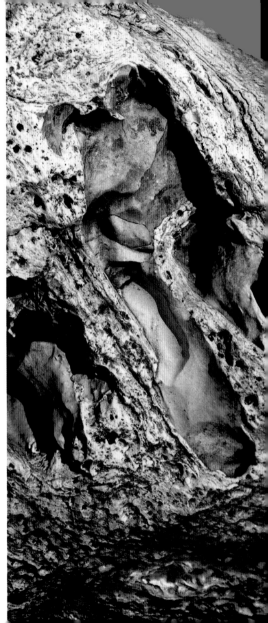

It is to see that every strutting politician, every world leader good and bad,
even our icons like every mortal man, shall one day be,
but a lost grain of sand on the face the earth.
For even if they were scattered here on this beach, amongst the sand,
they would be but one to a trillion.

For these rocks are more enduring, each is a portrait of lasting beauty
In harmony with nature,
the product of change that complements the needs of the earth
After each storm, I return in anticipation to see them uncovered again.
I marvel that such beauty lies hidden beneath the sand,
A world of colour and resilience uncovered by the mighty storm.
Here for a day or two is the hidden beauty of a thousand years in the making.
Always I discover yet another boulder of intricate colour and texture, all more
precious because soon the sand will be returned by the gentle waves.
Mysteriously the sand is back, the rocks have gone,
Yes, well before the summer, before the tired throngs of office workers, stressed
executives and fatigued professionals, join in with other New Zealanders and
their children.
They come to lie on their backs in the sun and swim in the surf,
oblivious to the rich treasure lying beneath the sand,
Just as I was so many years ago when I owned a beach front property,
but was too busy to enjoy it, and too tired to see
What is now revealed to me.

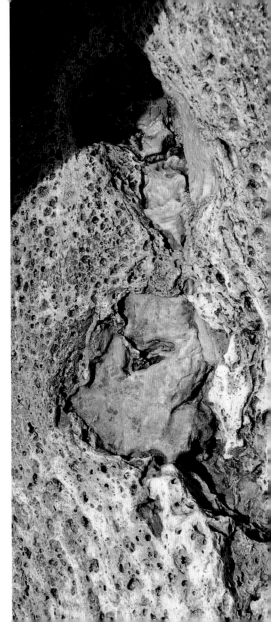

Children's Rock Poems

Mr Womble

Hallo Mr Womble, how do you feel when the boulders rumble and the rocks tumble?
I think of you in the storm, when other rocks are sad eyed and forlorn
You scurry around at night to see what the waves bring in but you are asleep again at dawn
I come to check that you are asleep as grandad says,
"You always nod off before we get out of bed."
He says you have lived here since before he was born.
I wish you would wake up at sunrise, and smile or open your eyes.
You must be really tired because you never move or even yawn.

Little Rock

Hallo Little Rock, you've been hiding under the sand.
Don't be frightened, this is your beach, and I care and understand.
I won't hurt you or take you away
because I will look forward to coming back and seeing you another day.

The Lion
at Our Beach

The man rang from the zoo
He said there is a lion escaped near you
He was in the circus in the town around
the bay.
He said, "Don't worry we always shoot a stray."

I was walking in the grass,
at the end of a beautiful Summers day
The men with guns had searched for a week,
now they'd gone away
They said the lion must have fallen down
the cliff onto the rocks below,
But they really didn't know.

Suddenly I saw him standing on the cliff
so proud and strong, but he did not go.
When he saw me he turned into a rock.
I knew then why the men could not find him,
Never again would he live behind iron bars
and hear the key turn in the lock
Every time he sees someone,
he turns into a tree or a rock.

Old Man Please Talk to Me

Old man of rock and sea,
please come and talk with me
There is so much that you could teach,
that is beyond the human reach.
How long have you sat there
with that pensive distant stare.
Watching sailing ships and canoes
Do you ever tire of those stunning views?
Have you been there ten thousand years?
What are your thoughts, do you harbour fears?
When I think of everyone alive today
When we are gone you'll still be looking out to sea
thank you, that simple fact talks to me.

Nature's Talks

Sitting here at Hahei on the beach at sunset,
once more in the classroom of nature,
I marvel at the colours of the rocks at low tide.
Some are above the gentle swell of the sea. Others are just below the surface.
I sit peacefully and let the peace and beauty of this natural world speak to me.

I also let my thoughts find me.
Then suddenly, it seems as if I have only just understood
one of nature's analogies about life.

The rocks that I love have something more to teach me.
It is simply this,
I now see that those rocks with such brilliance of texture and colour,
are only beautiful because of the life that they support.

Once again I see that both the rocks and the life they support are dependent
on the sea and the sun which complete the life giving cycle.

The rock is the foundation; the growth it supports is both
the children of the rock and the sea.
One gives a foundation for life,
For the other it is the harvest
because it is the water that nurtures by bringing nutrients.
As for all life on earth, water is essential
nevertheless, only part of the circle of inter dependency.

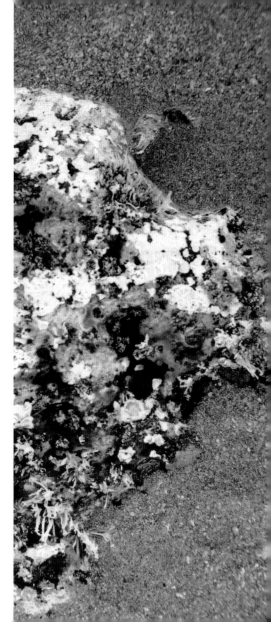

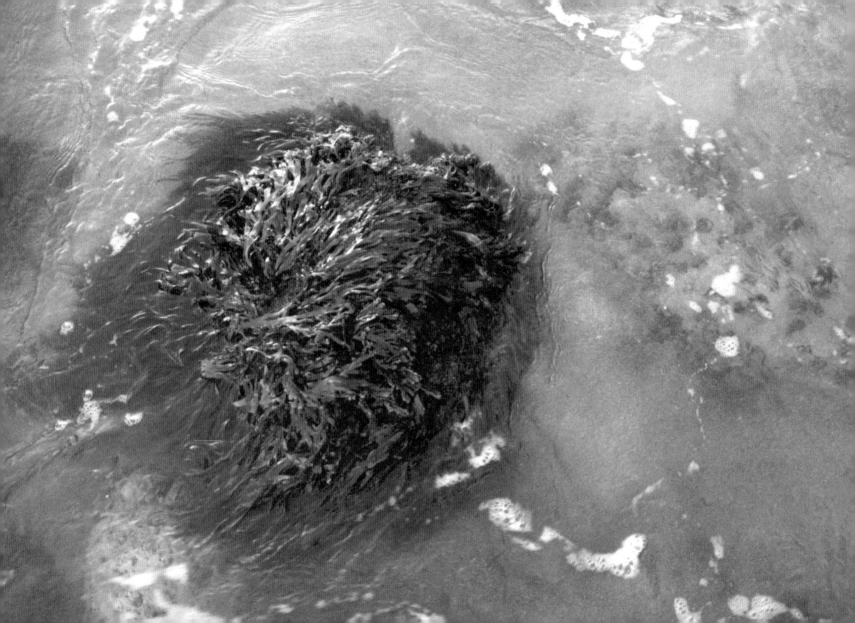

The natural world teaches that unless all living things live in harmony and balance,
life itself is denied.
I sit for a while longer and admire the textures
and the multiplicity of colour
blended by the subtle brush of nature.

As the sun sinks behind the hills the colours fade,
Nevertheless the subtlety of tones are beautiful and tranquil.

As twilight turns to dusk, I am reminded that it is the sun's warmth that sustains
the climate of growth and completes the essential balance that sustains life.

I sit and nature keeps talking to me,
I listen in silence and understand.
The rocks without the plant life would not have the depth of beauty:
The marine plants without the continual movement
and changing moods of the sea would dry out and die.
Without water on earth all life would die, yet it is only one part of the cycle.
Just as without the reliable visitation of the sun all life on earth
would be strangled by the vice grip of ice.

We are all alive because of these elements, this balance.
I saw once again the fundamental law of nature.
It requires that we all live in harmony with the natural world.
For indeed, don't plants convert carbon dioxide into oxygen for mankind?
Isn't our survival dependent on the fruit of the land and sea?
Just as our sensitivity, our peace of mind and joy of living
is nurtured by these elements.

As I walked back down the beach in darkness
I realised that this truth seems to be hidden from so many.

They race around in the mad pace of life creating and controlling,
by harvesting and utilising the natural resources of the world.
Yet they fail to pause and see that all around us the natural
world respects balance and inter dependency.
Without it our natural world would perish. And so would we.

Some would respond "Global trading and the breakdown of geographic barriers"
is surely illustrating the sharing of our resources, technology and co-operating
as a global village as never before.

The lesson for us is to see that like the rocks, our richness and character
comes from giving life to others from the depth of the human spirit,
not solely with the expectation of reward or profit.

We need to share more of our love, compassion and the richness of the human spirit.
Otherwise we ignore the underlying fragility of ethnic racial and political harmony.

Is this is not the underlying weakness of human nature that has resulted
in the death of over 200 million people this century as the result of wars alone.

As I write ethnic intolerance is rife.

To be willing to give and receive is the natural harmony of our existence.
To coexist in peace, to live and let live is the natural law of the earth.
If we care for our sons and daughters,
Is it not the greatest challenge that faces humanity?

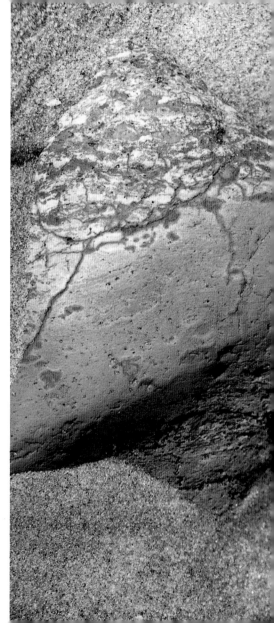

Dare to Love Again

Romantic Love

Is it wrong to have loved too much? Is romantic love only for fairy tales?
No! if you find it, enjoy it!
The harsh realities will creep upon us soon enough.
Then we may be left with just the memory and those classic words;
"It is better to have loved and lost than never to have loved at all"
Remembrance is the fragrance,
it forgives and forgets and adds its share of fantasy,
Taunting us with regret and deluding us with imaginings.
So this story is a desert wine enjoyed at the table of life,
adding to and being part of, the richness of memory.
In your cellar of memories you will have stored your own favourite desert wine.
Hence my story is everyone's story.
To reflect on love without indulging in excessive regret
is akin to a log fire on a cold night,
or the warmth of familiar company,
even though at moments it may elicit tears of sadness
and longing for that joy with a sweet sadness.
For to reflect on our ability to give and receive love
is to reflect on the beauty of the human spirit,
to accept its quality is owed to it's brevity.
When we come to accept this, we are able to be comfortable
with love's complex character. Only then are such memories akin to being
in the presence of an old and trusted friend. To know that you are about
to share things that are precious and understood.
This my friend, is the relationship between the mind and the heart.
On such occasions, when you meet, you feel their presence in your soul.

This Moment

This moment of all moments is the most precious.
It is opportunity waiting to be fulfilled.
It is the only reality that I possess.
Times gone, are unchangeable, the archives of my growth:
The leaves along my path.
What I do now corrects my errors along the way and shapes my future.
I will look to the future; plan for it, knowing it is like a guiding star
leading me on, nevertheless untouchable.

Summer Love

Today we awoke to the sound of waves

We lay in cotton sheets, lovers without guilt or regret.
Trust emerging, love growing.

Intense happiness has but a brief season
Pleasure must make room for reality.

A sudden parting, regret, realisation, too precious to lose
Beautiful feelings experienced in a New Zealand summer
Reality put on hold, then destiny's gift returned.
Denial
Musn't lose it.
Feeling is mutual, utter joy
Yes, I have to leave:
Of course I will come back!

Love kept alive by hope

Strengthened by memories
Taunted by fear
Desire put on hold
Waiting, waiting, waiting.

Promises in ink

The thrill of a letter hand-written,
Promises in ink.
Squiggles, inspired by love
empowered with emotion
Paper scented
Posted in haste
Hope alive
When will you arrive?

Missed connection, disbelief
The tomorrows have already begun
One faces winter alone haunted by what could have been
For the other, spring, reunions, old lovers, familiar friends.
For one it is a beginning, the other an end.
Hope dies a slow death.

Memories

When memories chill the evening sky
And I question the when and why
Your face haunts in brooding mist
Reminding me of what I've missed
Ah, regrets would line my coat
And choke the words in my throat.

It's then I'm drawn to the letters we once wrote
To remind myself that the source of such pain
Comes out of memories of what we gain.

Footprints in the Sand

We all know people who choose to hold on to sad memories.
They live in a world of footprints in the sand
Two going up the beach,
One set coming home from love out of reach.
People who live amongst broken dreams
Old love letters clutter the desk,
with half finished poems that can't express the grief.
People whom faith and hope failed to reach.
Grown men and women fighting despair, denied their lost love
Eyes rivetted to the rear vision mirror.
Living in a past that failed to teach.
Never happy with what today offers and longs to give.
Hearts captive to what they once had
They have forgotten how to live.

Eye to Eye

Relationships begin with eye contact and are over when eye contact ceases.
Love and feelings expressed through the eyes create the bond between two people.
The eyes are the most intimate form of expression, and the most honest.
The eyes display the inner feelings and emotions
There is one person you should never lose eye contact with.
It is your lover, for to do so is to break the vital communication.
It is to cease to know the heart and mind of the other.
With a lover it is to lose the intensity of feeling and the passion.

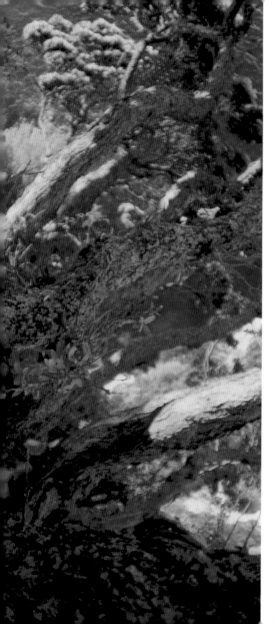

The Seed

The seed lying in the darkness of the soil.
I was never so alone, then I heard my spirit talking to my heart:
You are on your own but not alone,
The spirit of God's purpose broods in the air you breathe,
You were called for a purpose, but you also were given a free will,
You can choose to accept or reject your potential,
The choice is yours; there is before you an open door.
Just as the seed of the tallest tree began in the darkness of the soil,
The seed of your hope must begin in the soil of doubt and reasoning.
The seed of hope must be nurtured by faith, thought and speech.
Meditate on thoughts that are products of your faith.
In your quiet times tell yourself that it will come to pass.
Pray for destiny and timing to come together on your behalf.

The Pinnacle of Human Emotion

In the heart of each of us is a deep desire to be in love.
It may be well hidden. We may even deny it to ourselves.
Yet we cannot deny the utter joy of experiencing the wonderful feeling
of being in love equal to our romantic expectations.
We are born with this desire and ability to love.
It is the pinnacle of human emotion
When reciprocated, it is the lifeblood of pure joy
It turns winter into spring
It is to breathe the air of passion.
It is the closest we can return to the idealism of our youth.
It is the nearest we can come to bliss
When we are in love it is as if sunlight floods the dark corners of our mind,
which harbours fear and doubt, filling us with hope and assurance.'

Lead in the heart

To lose that love is to put lead in the heart and turn out the lights.
Everyday has the bleak chill of winter, the eye loses its sparkle and becomes
dulled by the dreadful realisation of loss, *remember, sometimes less is more.*
Every quiet moment is filled with regret.
It is as if day after day we are blanketed in a damp fog the sun cannot penetrate.
The artist in us is left with only two colours, black and the white.

Hence our creativity is no longer expressed with bright colours.
We often turn to the writer's pen to voice the pain of a wounded spirit
in song and prose. It is emotion set free.

Farewell

Farewell, this parting is intense
It is over, the incoming tide will remove all trace.
Destiny and timing do away with pretence
Two lovers eye to eye face to face,
Yet against separation there is no defence
Bitter sweet that last embrace
A final glimpse of the love in your beautiful face.

The moment you turn to leave a cord will snap.
Even though words will initially bridge the gap.

Email from a broken heart
Fact is, we are apart.

In a month reality has loosened love's grip.
The intensity and bond will slip.

I do not discount sweet words that follow.
However in time confessions of love are hollow.

Separation in time and space
Creates subtle changes in the human race.

The two people who a year before said goodbye
Professed undying love in that moment in time
It was their truth, neither told a lie
Memories supported by intent, and a lover's rhyme.

Such love suffers a slow and painful death and denial
There is always one who refuses to face the fact
Theirs is a long and painful trial
There is no curtain call, we cannot back track
Friends must listen and watch the final act
Be supportive and kind when lost love causes us to over-react

So decide early in life if you are willing to pay the price
Of maintaining a distant love affair.
Remember, joy goes to those who dare.
In parting, it is more often fate and destiny who toss the dice.
So on parting are you kinder to end it there.
It will save emotional energy and wasted time, each has its price.
Bitter loss and broken dreams make it harder next time to care.
But what is life without love to share?
Happiness comes to those who dare.

"Fear and doubt, being the ash that smothers the flame
Both need to be cleansed from our thoughts
For truth will protect us if we invite it to take its course"

"There is no reason for haste
But friendship, love and life
Should not be put on hold"

Doesn't Spring Always Follow Winter?

Nothing that is alive can remain frozen in time
Our lives have their seasons
Those that have loved and lost put aside the pain
And dare to love again.

Each partner is an intrinsic part of our being
Whether it is a glorious memory or a valuable lesson
Retain only the good memories and the lessons
Good memories are gifts held without fear.
Good memories improve with age, like the best wine
The good times we spend with another can never be taken away.
They are ours forever.

For those who have loved and lost, remember your need to love again.
In your heart lies the seed of love.
For love is the child of the human heart.
love is the vibrant release of a positive energy
It enriches our life while empowering us and those we love.
It adds vibrant colour to our landscape.
It is good for our health and self esteem.

There is Purpose in Solitude

Remember too that after each relationship there is a time when your emotions
need to lie fallow. Just as the soil needs rest after producing a crop.
Note how the freshly ploughed earth is regenerated by the rain and sun.
Where love is lost in painful regret, your tears were necessary.
to wash away the acidity of broken trust, crushed hope and bitter loss.
Your tears soften and penetrate the hard exterior of the seed,
Yes, the seed of love is still lying in your heart.
However you can never truly love again until bitterness is bleached from its soil.
This is a time for reflection, to recognise lessons learned
Otherwise we are prone to repeat them.
Only through acknowledging the lesson can past hurts disappear.

Stepping Stones or Stumbling Blocks

We then can concede, that two imperfect people tried and lessons were learnt
Then we must determine to make stepping stones out of stumbling blocks.
Yes, mistakes are stepping stones, when the lesson is learnt.

Past relationships are the vital steps to a successful relationship.
Past relationships are the leaves along our path.
They fertilise our understanding.
Only then are we ready to love again
Acknowledge past traits that make you vulnerable
to compromise and control.

Loving Again Begins With Forgiveness

Know also that you can never truly love others with confidence
until you forgive others and yourself.
Protective cynicism is a normal protective mechanism
However cynicism should never be blatant or expressed openly
It is like the ashes that smother the flame.
As the proverb teaches.

"Be as gentle as a dove but as wise as a serpent."

Your Most Precious Gift

If you have the capacity to love and trust again,
You hold within your heart the most precious of human gifts.

A new love is like the sun at the end of a long winter.
In the spring it appears taunting and full of promise.
Then as we dare to trust and love again
our hearts become warmer encouraging the tender leaves to unfold.

Your intrinsic belief in yourself and your willingness to show love and compassion
is like a lamp in the window for those lost in darkness and despair.

By sharing this gift we have discovered an essential ingredient to a happy life
Therefore be wise and cautious but dare to love again.